AF433356

My Protector, My Protected

by

Amber Steffens

A Love That Cannot Be

Feeling numb to the affections you give
My heart numb to the things you mention
Actions are loud and yours have said
That you don't care about my worries or pains
I show concern and give you my world
You toss it aside for feelings in a bottle
That bottle you keep ever so close
Drove a wedge between what you wanted most
My heart is now ice and no longer yours
Because you chose items you needed most
I tried to speak to reason and beg
To deaf ears you feigned to not see
That now that I am numb you try to convey
Those feelings of love and actions I needed
Before when that bottle was all you wanted
No longer so dumb and no longer that girl
Who willingly succumbs to your empty words.
I thought I loved what I saw in you
Turns out I loved what I thought I knew
I fell for the you you can no longer be
Loving the past can hurt so much worse
Then being blind to the present and forcing yourself
To feel a love that can no longer be.

Beauty is

Beauty isn't the eyes, hair, or looks
Beauty isn't the things I have the most.
Beauty isn't the clothes that I adore
Beauty isn't the car I can afford
Beauty does not come from what I take
Beauty is what I can make
I can make you smile
I can make your day
I can make you know that it's okay
I can make you cheer
I can make you laugh

Blessing

Caring for another is such a joy
Like another job without the pay
Though what you loose in coin and trade
Gets gained in affection games and mess
Though chores increase and so does stress
You couldn't trade what you gain
The love of one who needs you most
Is a blessing that you chose
Loving another and giving them
All your moments though not all the best
You struggle together and learn to live
In the happy moments with cheers and grins
And the moments when you want to give in
This isn't a job that pays with coin
Nor do you vacation days off or breaks
But even still we wouldn't want
To miss the smiles and cheers
Nor the anger and tears
The kisses so sweet and sometimes sticky
To peering in the corners for something scary
Having a fight because they think they are right
To the punishments given to give them sight
Having a blast playing and laughing!
To kissing away the pain and calming
You wouldn't want to miss a thing
Nor the song that blessing will sing.

Daggers You Speak

Overwhelmed by the feeling of being watched
Being judged for merely being you
Unable to escape the words that are hissed
Venomous accusations tossed your way
Unable to hide away as you creak
Mentally breaking but trying to hide
How deep it hurts to be harmed by those smiles
Fake friendships suddenly in view
You fall and creak pieces crumble off
As you smile at the ones who harmed you
Unwilling to show them the pain they caused
Keep it locked until, alone, you may show
What hard those daggers had done.

Day We Miss

There is a day for us all
That we think of with wonder
If you had never been
What could we have seen?
Would we be the same as we are
What would have changed within
Could we smile without thinking
That the world is out to get us
Would we smile with joy.
And not just because we have too
Would we be able to let others see
The us we keep hidden.
This day of ours that taunts us
This day that is forbidden
Comes at us once a year
Always repeating
We always remember
Though we don't wish
The day that brings with it
Our memories we most miss

Did You Know

Did you know a hand could be so warm,
Or a kiss could melt away the storm inside.
Did you know hugs and cuddles
Can turn worries to puddles.
Did you know feeling how they love
Can make your world sore like a dove.
Did you know their voice so sweet and kind
Can make you smile and not mind
Not mind the mischief they spin
A distraction from what's inside
Did you know that no matter
You need that small light
So much more then you know.
That bundle of joy and love
Is the world you searched for
Is the joy and love
You needed in your darkest.

Endless Prison

Staring at the endless sky
I stop and wonder why
Why does the world seem so big
And yet when alone with the voices within
It seems so small and condemned.
Scratching at the doors to your own isolation
 and yet unable to free yourself from the chains of your own
demons.
Looking up again you see the wide open sky glaring at you.
Taunting your helpless state.
Knowing your own chains bind you
Slowly changing yourself into something new or otherwise
forgotten
In the endless void changing the never ending canvas of
negativity
To an endlessly beautiful and glowing sky above.
Rising above your own prison
Chains rust and fade as you slowly learn to stand.
The once heavy doors that wouldn't move slowly push
themselves opened
A once compressed life now able to breath and feel the wind as
you look on into that beautiful endless green.

Endless Sky

Endless sea of blue above
With soft waves of white gently rolling by
Watching as they dance and play
Smiling you watch feeling so sure of things
Smile fades seeing how the world fades
Endless sea of blue changes
The blue a darkening grey to black
Soft whites now grays and swirling
Smile fades as the turmoil twists and moves
Curling up hands over your ears screaming
As what you knew so well and was so sure of
Is no longer so, confusion anger
What do you feel your endless sky so angry
Screaming like the storm above
What you knew seems so distant and past
That storm inside no longer within your control
Forgetting how to bring back that soft sky you crave.

Motivation ticking by

Laying here watching the clock tick by
Slowly but ever moving minute to hour
Endless tasks that are needed but
Motivation just faded
I move up from my spot wishing to act
But lying back feels more aided
Needing to move and needing to go
But feeling so low body feeling of lead
Knowing what you need to do
Yet drowning Inside unable to go
The ocean inside demands that you remain
Held down by nothing but your own chains
Chains made from the pressure you made
Breathing and fighting the chains until
The ocean you made is to deep to deal
No longer able to swim through the thoughts
You allow yourself to drown and be lost.
Until you find the strength to fight your way up.
Changing your thoughts and changing your mind.
Maybe what saves you from that ocean of demise.

Pretending to be

People around you going about their day.
Talking and laughing as you fade away.
No one notices the lack of joy in your eye
Or the way you gently walk by
No one sees how alone you feel or act.
No one cares because they are part of a pack
A pack who talks and laughs and goes about their lives.
While your trying so hard not to cry.
Protecting yourself with an act
Slip on your mask no one will see.
That broken you you lock away with a key
We don't want your sadness or your tears
No one cares about your fears.
Just smile and wave with an I'm okay
And they continue about their day.
No one cares what's behind the mask
No one wonders what's inside
The outside is what they all see
The smiles and joy you pretend to be
Is all they care to see

Remembering You

Staying up late watching our show
With our diet soda on the table
Ice creams being taken two by two
Smiling and laughing and shushing those
Who would ruin the moment that we hold
Cuddled in the blanket staying up late
I could tell you everything my secret you kept
Books I adored you gave them to me
Helping me with what all that I had passion
Taking us out doors to explore
Swimming at night in the pool just outside
Catching frogs and telling him to let us play
He didn't know us the way that you did
He doesn't understand the bond we kept.
Over the years your still on my mind
With all my heart I miss your being
With all my thoughts I miss the memories
We didn't get to make since you had to go
Taken so soon you were so young
A mere thirty five with so much to give
Dyed blonde hair that I will never forget
And a smile that shown with mischief
Soft green eyes that changed with your mood
I should know because mine do too.
I miss you so much you will never know
That I love you more then I can show
 My daughter is like you stubborn and strong.
She shares your name though her middle is where
I honored you so she will always know

That her grandmother is with her
Though you never met.
I will love you forever and never forget
That you are my protector my mother and parent.

Stranger I Once Knew

Watching as those you once knew disappear
Thinking you understood who they were and they to you
Suddenly talking and laughing among yourselves feels so queer,
unknown,
Like strangers in a room
Who are these faces that you thought you knew so well.
A stranger with the mask of a friend.
Their words muffled, as if under water
Their actions foreign, as if unknown
What you had can no longer be
Strangers in familiar faces
No longer the comfort you knew
And things between you close
Like you are nothing anymore.

Ticking on by

Tick tick tick tick
Everything moves at the beat of a tick
Tick tick tick tick
Wake up get dressed
Drink coffee move along.
Run some errands go to work
Tick tick tick tick
Come home cook and clean.
Lay down repeat.
This world but an endless clock
Never ending always a reputation

Winds That Motivate

Moving in the breeze the windmill turns
Helped along the blades gently pushed
As they turn the light on top shines
Like the windmill we also rely
On the ones who gently stand behind
Pushing us to be more then we can alone
The light blinks when those we leaned on
No longer move our blades so gentle
Instead our blades start to turn slowly
The winds that moved and kept us going
That kept the blades gently blowing
Stop that soft and kind encouraging
And make those blades move ever slower.
And soon before you know it
Those blades stop
The breeze still
No longer do they spin and move
No longer are the blades pushed through
No longer are those we need
Behind to be our breeze
So the blades we are
No longer move

Wishes For Her

Strange as it is I can see what I wish
My desires are something that seem amiss
Wishing so much for such simple things
People would think are silly dreams
I wish for my health to not deplete
Hoping for my life to remain stable
I wish my loves wishes to be complete.
For she is young and very able.
I wish for enough to get us on by
So that we can continue to survive
I wish for her joy happiness and cheer
I long to see her swore far from here
I wish for my love to know her own worth
For she deserves all the world and much more
I wish for a day when I can safely say
That I did my best for both our sakes.
I wish no more then her to smile.
For she is my world and my child.

Within Oneself

Buried under the pressure I see the clutter
But my body of lead refuses to utter
Knowing the things I must complete
But my mind says it's only a feat
Something so minor we don't need complete
But I know inside it's important
I get up from the place I laid all day
Only be drained by so little an act
The cleaning can wait
The chores in my mind are so minor
But yet so important I rise up
Only to remember something I had forgotten
Thinking it's okay to wait
The tasks I need will not fade
Once more where I had been all day
 I wish I could be different But
I feel like I'll never over come
That intense feeling of dread
That comes from being a prisoner
Within myself

World Gone Cold

Ground is shaking
Mind is racing
The venom you speak
And the pain I feel.
Everything is done to spite
Things are taken to light
Loyalty placed in the wrong
Self persevere no longer strong
Work becomes your home
And home only a place to lay.
Giving your all for the pay
Family no longer first.
When work becomes your all
You have already given up
What truly matters
In this world gone cold

More Like family

We've been friends for so many years,
Through the fighting and tears
Distance doesn't make us any less close
You are truly who I trust the most.
We've both suffered losses and pains
But we've both had smiles laughs and gains
Though we met online it seems
We are closer then just mere friends.
I enjoy the days we talk and complain.
I feel more like a sister instead
I'm glad that through art I found someone
That I can be with as just myself
I'm glad that we met you are truly a blessing
Though we met through the web I can honestly say
That meeting you Vicki has made my year, week, and day.
Thank you for all that you do
Honesty though sometimes brutal
Just shows how close to you I am

My Protector, My Protected

by

Amber Steffens

Dedication

I'd like to thank my daughter Allison, best friend Marisa, and best friend who feels more like a sister Vicki.

Allison for always giving me the strength to get over the bumps in the road.

Marisa D'Amato who made the stunning book cover and has been a dear friend for years.

Vicki Rybka for being a close friend who has been there through most of my life's struggles and always given me the best advice and the best lectures when needed.

I love you all and I thank you so much every day.

About The Author

Amber Steffens is a young woman living in southern Kentucky.
She has always had a passion for reading books of most genres.
She is also an accomplished artist who enjoys writing and
spending quality time with her daughter.

Look for these other great titles from Zombie Media

Loving Bigfoot
Haunted Harlan County Vol.1
The Leaf Lady at the Amber Estates
True Short Stories of the Paranormal: My Personal Experiences
Buried Treasures
Understanding Bigfoot
The Road to Leadville
Bigfoot Witness
My Haunted House and other Weird Tales
I saw a UFO: Mysteries of the sky
Bigfoot and Eastern Cousins
Sasquatch Family Ties
The Ivory-billed Woodpecker:Taunting Extinction

Available on Amazon and other fine retailers